A Comprehensive Account of the Nuclear Disaster

Oliver Lancaster

Published by Oliver Lancaster, 2023.

A COMPREHENSIVE ACCOUNT OF THE NUCLEAR DISASTER

First edition. June 27, 2023.

Copyright © 2023 Oliver Lancaster.

ISBN: 979-8215184806

Written by Oliver Lancaster.

Sign up to my free newsletter to get updates on new releases, FREE teaser chapters to upcoming releases and FREE digital short stories.

Or visit https://tinyurl.com/olanc

I never spam and you can unsubscribe at any time.

Disclaimer

This book is intended to provide a comprehensive and insightful overview of the Chernobyl nuclear disaster based on available information up to the date of publication. While every effort has been made to ensure the accuracy of the details within, some minor discrepancies may exist due to varying accounts or ongoing developments.

The authors and publishers have taken considerable care in creating this narrative, but they make no warranties, express or implied, with respect to the completeness or accuracy of the contents of this book and specifically disclaim any implied warranties of merchantability or fitness for a particular purpose. They shall not be held liable or responsible to any person or entity with respect to any loss or incidental or consequential damages caused, or alleged to have been caused, directly or indirectly, by the information contained in this book.

Chernobyl: Unveiling the Tragedy - A Comprehensive Account of the Nuclear Disaster

A COMPREHENSIVE ACCOUNT OF THE NUCLEAR DISASTER

Introduction to Chernobyl: Setting the Stage

Long before the name 'Chernobyl' became associated with one of the world's worst nuclear disasters, it was just a small city located in the northern reaches of Ukraine. It was a name that resonated with the harmonious rhythm of ordinary life, as commonplace in Ukraine as Springfield or Madison might be in the United States. This quiet city lay in the shadow of the enormous Chernobyl Nuclear Power Plant, a monument to the wonders of modern technological advancement and the power of the atom.

Chernobyl, whose name in Ukrainian folklore signifies a bitter, black, and poisonous weed, was an ironically fitting name for a city that would become synonymous with one of humanity's most devastating technological failures.

Geographically, Chernobyl is situated in the heart of Europe, on the fertile plains of the Pripyat River, approximately 130 kilometers north of Ukraine's capital, Kyiv. The city is enveloped by a beautiful landscape that, for centuries, has been a rich tapestry of forests, marshes, and farmland.

Historically, Chernobyl has roots that stretch back to the 12th century. It was a vibrant city that had seen the ebb and flow of empires, witnessing the grandeur of the Czars and the hardships of war. Throughout this time, its people maintained a deep connection with the land, passing down stories, traditions, and a love of their city through generations. But as the wheels of progress turned, this idyllic landscape was chosen for a grand experiment in harnessing nuclear power.

The Chernobyl Nuclear Power Plant, a few kilometers north of the city, was more than just a power station. It was a testament to the might of the Soviet Union and its ambitious nuclear power program. The plant housed four RBMK-1000 reactors, a type of light-water, graphite-moderated reactor that was the pride of Soviet engineering. In fact, when it was constructed in the 1970s, it was the largest nuclear power plant in Europe. These reactors were designed to produce both plutonium for the nation's weapons program and electricity for the burgeoning Ukrainian population.

A symbol of progress and modernity, the plant was presented to the world as an icon of the USSR's technological prowess. It was seen as a beacon of scientific achievement that promised not just power, but the glory of a brighter future. Little did the world know that this shining beacon was perched on the edge of a precipice, and that its fall would cast a long and deadly shadow across the globe.

The Chernobyl Nuclear Power Plant was a complex, sophisticated piece of technology, emblematic of mankind's capacity to harness the forces of nature. However, like all technologies, it was only as safe as the systems and processes that were in place to control and regulate it. The human element, too, played a significant role in the running of this mammoth plant. And as we will see, it was this combination of technology, process, and human decision-making that would set the stage for a tragedy of unimaginable proportions.

With this background in mind, the stage is set for the unfolding of an unprecedented nuclear tragedy that had far-reaching implications. As we delve into the subsequent chapters of this story, it's important to remember that Chernobyl, this quiet city by the Pripyat River, was much more than just the site of a nuclear disaster. It was a place of history, of lives lived and lost, and a place forever altered by the invisible specter of radiation. But more importantly, Chernobyl is a potent reminder of the human cost of ambition unchecked by caution.

OLIVER LANCASTER

Chapter 1: The Chernobyl Nuclear Power Plant: Design and Functionality

The Construction and Structure of the Chernobyl Nuclear Power Plant

The Chernobyl Nuclear Power Plant, known in its time as the V.I. Lenin Nuclear Power Station, was more than just a utilitarian structure. It was a potent symbol of Soviet might and technological prowess. Rising out of the flat, fertile Ukrainian landscape, the plant was a marvel of concrete, steel, and ambition. The construction of such a colossal structure was not just a formidable engineering challenge but also a testament to the immense resources and manpower that the Soviet Union was willing to invest in its nuclear dream.

Construction of the power plant began in the 1970s, with the first reactor, Reactor No. 1, going online in 1977. It was followed by the completion of Reactor No. 2 in 1978, No. 3 in 1981, and No. 4 in 1983. The power plant was designed to house a total of six reactors; at the time of the disaster in 1986, Reactors No. 5 and 6 were still under construction.

Each of these reactors was of a design known as the RBMK-1000, a high-power channel-type reactor that used graphite as a moderator and was cooled by light water. This was a unique design used primarily in the Soviet Union, touted for its ability to be refueled while still in operation and for its capacity to produce both electricity and plutonium for military purposes.

A defining characteristic of the RBMK-1000 reactor was its enormous size. Each reactor was housed in a massive concrete and steel structure that towered over the surrounding landscape. The reactor's core contained nearly 1700 individual fuel channels, each surrounded by a graphite moderator. A coolant of light water circulated around these channels, absorbing the heat generated by the nuclear reactions taking place within the fuel rods.

The RBMK-1000 design did not include a large, robust containment structure, a common safety feature in most other nuclear reactor designs worldwide. These containment structures are designed to contain radioactive materials in the event of a nuclear accident. Instead, the Chernobyl plant's reactors were encased in a more lightweight structure often referred to as the "biological shield," which was primarily designed to protect workers from radiation during normal operation.

The power plant's design also included several other distinctive features. These included a unique positive void coefficient, which essentially means that if the water coolant turned into steam (creating a 'void'), it would increase the reaction rate in the reactor. This could potentially lead to a dangerous increase in power output. The control rods, designed to absorb neutrons and slow the nuclear reaction, were tipped with graphite, a material that initially increased the reaction rate before slowing it down. This design was meant to improve the efficiency of the reactor but under certain conditions, could contribute to instability.

In total, the Chernobyl Nuclear Power Plant was a formidable symbol of the Soviet Union's industrial and technological capabilities. Its towering silos, vast turbine halls, and maze of pipes and machinery were representative of a nation's ambition to conquer the atom and harness its power for the good of its people. Yet, it was within this monument to progress that the seeds of one of mankind's greatest disasters were sown, a stark reminder of the potentially dire consequences when our reach exceeds our grasp.

The RBMK Reactor: An Explanation of its Features

The RBMK reactor, an acronym derived from Russian which translates to 'High Power Channel-Type Reactor', is a type of nuclear fission reactor that was unique to the Soviet Union. It was one of the mainstays of their nuclear power program and the Chernobyl Nuclear Power Plant was a primary example of its use. Understanding the design and workings of the RBMK reactor is integral to grasping the sequence of events that led to the Chernobyl disaster.

At its core, the RBMK was a light-water-cooled, graphite-moderated pressure tube design. This means it used normal water as a coolant and solid graphite as a moderator. A moderator in a nuclear reactor slows down neutrons, which allows them to be captured by uranium-235 atoms and continue the nuclear fission chain reaction.

A distinct feature of the RBMK design was its use of individual fuel channels, rather than a single pressure vessel, which is common in most other types of reactors. Each reactor had about 1,700 fuel channels that held uranium fuel rods. These channels, arranged in a cylindrical configuration, passed through the graphite moderator block.

The reactor was designed to allow the fuel channels to be refueled while it was still operating. In contrast, most other reactor designs required shutdown during refueling. This was a significant operational advantage of the RBMK design, as it allowed for continuous electricity production.

One of the most significant and controversial design features of the RBMK reactor was its positive void coefficient. This is a technical term which means that if the water coolant in the reactor were to turn into steam (or 'void'), the nuclear reaction rate within the reactor would increase. In simpler terms, more steam meant more reactivity, which could potentially lead to an uncontrollable increase in power. Most other reactors are designed with a negative void coefficient, where the formation of steam decreases the reaction rate, adding an inherent layer of safety.

The control rods in the RBMK reactors had another distinctive feature. These rods, made of neutron-absorbing material, were designed to be inserted into the reactor to slow or halt the nuclear reaction. In the RBMK reactors, however, the tips of these rods were made of graphite, the same material used as a moderator in the reactor. The insertion of the rods displaced coolant and momentarily increased the reaction rate in the lower part of the reactor due to the graphite tips, before the absorber part of the rods could slow the reaction. Under certain conditions, this could create a localized increase in power, adding a risk factor to an already unstable situation.

Perhaps the most criticized aspect of the RBMK design was the lack of a robust containment structure. Most nuclear reactors worldwide are equipped with a substantial containment structure, a shell of concrete and steel meant to contain the release of radioactive materials in the event of an accident. The RBMK reactors, including those at Chernobyl, were instead housed in a relatively light structure which was not designed to withstand a significant explosion or contain a major release of radioactive material.

While the RBMK design did have some benefits, such as its capacity for continuous operation and plutonium production, its unique features also made it susceptible to instability under certain conditions. Combined with operational and regulatory shortcomings, these design features contributed to the disaster that would unfold at the Chernobyl nuclear power plant.

OLIVER LANCASTER

Chapter 2: The Events Leading to Disaster: A Chain of Mistakes

An Overview of the Events Leading Up to the Chernobyl Disaster

The Chernobyl disaster was not a singular event caused by a singular mistake. Rather, it was the result of a complex series of actions, decisions, and miscalculations that culminated in a tragedy that resonates to this day.

The fateful sequence of events began on April 25, 1986, a day before the explosion. Reactor 4 of the Chernobyl Nuclear Power Plant was scheduled to be shut down for routine maintenance. This shutdown provided an opportunity to conduct a test that had been planned but postponed several times before. The test aimed to determine whether the turbines could provide sufficient power to run the cooling pumps in the event of a loss of main electrical power supply, a scenario that could occur during a plant shutdown or an external power outage. This was a critical safety test, designed to enhance the plant's overall safety protocol.

The test was supposed to be carried out earlier in the day by an experienced day-shift crew, but several delays resulted in a significant postponement. By the time all systems were ready for the test, the evening shift was on duty. This crew had not been prepared to conduct the test, yet they were instructed to carry it out regardless.

As the reactor was being powered down in preparation for the test, its power levels fell more than intended, reaching a near-shutdown state. However, the decision was made to continue with the test despite the reactor's unstable state at such low power levels.

The operators then removed a large number of control rods from the reactor core to increase its power. The removal of these rods brought the reactor to an extremely unstable condition, but this was not fully understood by the operators at the time.

At 1:23 AM on April 26, the test commenced. The reactor's emergency cooling system was intentionally turned off to simulate a power loss scenario. When the test finally began, and the turbines were disconnected from the reactor, the power level began to increase.

Realizing that the power surge could become uncontrollable, the operators attempted to shut down the reactor by inserting all the control rods. However, due to the reactor's design, the graphite tips of the control rods initially displaced coolant and increased the reaction rate, leading to a rapid power surge.

Within a matter of seconds, the power level spiked, and the fuel channels ruptured, leading to a series of explosions. The roof of the reactor building was blown off, and a plume of highly radioactive dust and debris was released into the atmosphere.

This chain of events leading to the Chernobyl disaster was not solely due to the errors made during that fatal night. The disaster was also a culmination of design flaws in the RBMK reactor, inadequate safety culture, lack of comprehensive regulations, and insufficient operator training. The tragedy of Chernobyl serves as a stark reminder of how the intersection of human error, design flaw, and systemic negligence can lead to catastrophic consequences.

The Flawed Reactor Design and Safety Measures

While human errors undeniably played a significant role in the Chernobyl disaster, these errors occurred within a broader context of flawed reactor design and inadequate safety measures. Understanding these flaws provides critical insight into why the disaster happened and how it could have been prevented.

The first critical flaw lay within the very heart of the Chernobyl plant—the RBMK-1000 reactor. As highlighted earlier, this reactor type had several unique characteristics that contributed to the disaster. Among them was the reactor's positive void coefficient. In practical terms, this meant that an increase in steam (or 'voids') in the reactor could lead to a rapid and uncontrollable increase in power. This characteristic made the reactor inherently unstable under certain operating conditions.

In addition to this, the RBMK reactor was designed to allow refueling while still operating, which resulted in a more complex and less stable core configuration. The sheer size of the reactor, with its 1700 individual fuel channels, also made the reactor more challenging to control and monitor.

Another crucial design flaw was the nature of the control rods. The graphite-tipped control rods, meant to absorb neutrons and control the reactor's power, could temporarily increase the power output in certain parts of the reactor when they were first inserted. This design defect was a key contributor to the power surge that led to the reactor's explosion.

The lack of a robust containment structure was another significant design flaw. Most nuclear reactors are built with a solid containment structure, designed to prevent the release of radioactive materials in the event of a reactor breach. The Chernobyl reactors were instead enclosed in a relatively light structure, which was incapable of containing the explosion that occurred.

Beyond these design flaws, there were also serious shortcomings in the safety measures and procedures at the Chernobyl plant. The plant's operators were not fully trained or prepared to manage the reactor in the conditions that led up to the accident. The safety test that precipitated the disaster was not properly coordinated or communicated, with critical safety protocols being bypassed.

At the systemic level, there was a lack of a strong safety culture within the Soviet nuclear industry. This was evident in the failure to learn from past incidents and near misses, and the lack of transparency and open communication about potential risks and issues. Safety concerns raised about the RBMK reactor design following previous incidents were not adequately addressed, and plant operators were not fully informed of these issues.

The Chernobyl disaster was a tragic confluence of flawed reactor design, inadequate safety measures, and operational mistakes. It stands as a stark reminder of the potential consequences of ignoring or underestimating safety risks in the pursuit of technological progress.

Chapter 3: April 26, 1986: The Catastrophic Explosion

The Explosion and Immediate Aftermath

In the early morning hours of April 26, 1986, as the ill-fated safety test was being carried out, Reactor 4 of the Chernobyl Nuclear Power Plant experienced a rapid power surge. This dramatic increase in power led to a sequence of events that culminated in a catastrophic explosion.

At 1:23:45 AM, the operators of Reactor 4 engaged the emergency shutdown system, intending to insert all control rods to halt the nuclear reaction. However, due to the reactor's design, the insertion of the graphite-tipped control rods initially displaced coolant and increased the reactor's power output.

The sudden and intense power surge caused fuel pellets in the reactor to explode, rupturing the fuel channels. This was immediately followed by a steam explosion, which destroyed the reactor core and caused the 1000-tonne upper plate of the reactor to be blown off. This initial explosion was followed by a second, even more powerful explosion only a few seconds later.

The force of these explosions obliterated the reactor and set the building's roof on fire. The upper biological shield of the reactor was thrown upward and then fell back onto the reactor, smashing through the remaining construction and further spreading radioactive material.

These explosions sent a plume of radioactive particles into the atmosphere, some of which fell back onto the plant and its immediate surroundings, while the rest was carried by the wind over a vast geographical area. An intense fire began in the graphite moderator of the reactor, which was exposed to the atmosphere by the explosion. This fire sent a plume of highly radioactive smoke and dust into the sky, which spread fallout over a large area.

In the immediate aftermath of the explosion, the plant's operators and the emergency workers, now known as liquidators, were faced with a crisis of an unprecedented scale. Despite the extreme danger, many of them stayed at or returned to the reactor to fight the fires and try to manage the situation.

The Soviet government initially tried to downplay the incident, not evacuating the nearby town of Pripyat until about 36 hours after the explosion. When the evacuation order finally came, residents were told it would be a temporary measure lasting only about three days. Most left their belongings behind, expecting to return shortly. They would never return.

The days following the explosion saw a desperate struggle to contain the spread of radiation and prevent further explosions. This involved tasks like pouring sand and boron onto the reactor from helicopters to try to smother the fire and limit the spread of radioactive particles.

These initial response efforts were characterized by immense courage and self-sacrifice but were also marked by confusion and misinformation. The full scale of the disaster was not immediately understood by the responders, many of whom received lethal doses of radiation.

The explosion at Chernobyl and its immediate aftermath would prove to be a turning point in our understanding of nuclear safety, with the lessons learned from this catastrophe continuing to shape the industry to this day.

Initial Response and Efforts to Control the Situation

The immediate aftermath of the Chernobyl disaster was characterized by confusion, uncertainty, and a desperate scramble to control an unprecedented and rapidly escalating nuclear crisis. While the explosion's seismic shock waves registered on nearby instruments, it took some time before the extent of the catastrophe began to be comprehended.

At 1:45 AM, less than half an hour after the explosion, firefighters from the nearby town of Pripyat were dispatched to the scene. They arrived to a devastating sight: the reactor building was severely damaged, its roof was aflame, and radioactive debris was strewn across the surrounding area. These brave individuals, unaware of the lethal levels of radiation, began the harrowing task of combating the fires. Many of them succumbed to acute radiation sickness in the weeks that followed.

Meanwhile, the plant management was struggling to understand the situation. Initial inspections by plant workers and firefighters reported that the reactor was intact, a grave misinterpretation driven partly by disbelief that such a catastrophic failure could occur. The true nature of the disaster was only realized several hours later when it became clear that the reactor was completely destroyed.

In the early morning hours, a government commission was created to manage the response to the accident. Led by Valery Legasov, First Deputy Director of the Kurchatov Institute of Atomic Energy, and Boris Shcherbina, a deputy chairman of the Soviet Council of Ministers, the commission arrived at Chernobyl by helicopter on the evening of April 26.

Their first major task was the immediate evacuation of Pripyat, the town nearest to the power plant, inhabited primarily by plant workers and their families. The evacuation order was given on April 27, more than 24 hours after the explosion. The residents were told they would be away for only a few days. As history would have it, they would never return.

Simultaneously, efforts were made to contain the radioactive materials and put out the fires. Helicopters flown by military pilots started dumping sand, clay, boron, and lead onto the reactor, in an attempt to smother the blaze and limit the spread of radioactive particles. Over the following days, nearly 5,000 metric tons of material would be dropped onto the reactor site.

Another significant concern was a potential thermal explosion. It was feared that the molten nuclear fuel could melt through the reactor floor and come into contact with the water in the flooded basement, causing a steam explosion that could further spread radioactive contamination. Three plant workers, often referred to as the "Chernobyl divers," volunteered to drain the water, successfully averting a second catastrophe.

While these initial efforts played a significant role in managing the immediate crisis, they also exposed a large number of individuals to high levels of radiation. The lack of appropriate protective equipment and the sheer magnitude of the radioactive exposure led to severe health consequences for many of these early responders, illustrating the profound human cost of the disaster.

OLIVER LANCASTER

Chapter 4: The Invisible Enemy: Understanding Radiation

Different Types of Radiation and Their Effects on the Human Body

In order to understand the scale and severity of the Chernobyl disaster, it's necessary to explore the nature of radiation and its effects on the human body. The term "radiation" refers to energy that is emitted from a source and travels through space or a material medium. In the context of a nuclear disaster like Chernobyl, the focus is on ionizing radiation, which carries enough energy to remove tightly bound electrons from atoms, thus creating ions.

Ionizing radiation comes in several forms, each with its unique properties and effects on human health:

1. Alpha Particles: Alpha particles are heavy and carry a double positive charge. They don't penetrate very far into matter and can be stopped by a sheet of paper or human skin. However, if alpha-emitting substances are ingested or inhaled, they can cause significant damage, since they are highly ionizing and can damage the cells and tissues of organs directly.

2. Beta Particles: Beta particles are much smaller than alpha particles and carry a single negative charge. They can penetrate further than alpha particles—through skin and into the underlying tissues—but can be stopped by a thin sheet of metal or plastic. Like alpha particles, if beta-emitting substances enter the body, they can damage cells and tissues.

3. Gamma Rays: Gamma rays are a form of electromagnetic radiation, similar to X-rays but with much higher energy. They are deeply penetrating and can pass through several centimeters of lead or meters of concrete. Gamma rays are a significant concern in a nuclear disaster because they can irradiate the whole body and damage cells throughout the body, leading to radiation sickness or long-term health effects.

4. Neutrons: Neutrons are uncharged particles that can travel great distances and penetrate all types of matter. They can make other materials radioactive, a process known as neutron activation. Neutrons are a particular concern in the immediate vicinity of a nuclear reactor or a nuclear explosion.

When the human body is exposed to high levels of ionizing radiation, it can cause a range of health effects. The severity of these effects depends on the type and amount of radiation exposure, the duration of exposure, and the specific parts of the body exposed.

Acute radiation sickness, also known as radiation syndrome, can occur after exposure to a high dose of radiation over a short period. Symptoms may include nausea, vomiting, headache, and diarrhea. High doses can also cause skin burns, acute hair loss, and damage to the bone marrow, leading to a decrease in white blood cells and an increased risk of infection.

Long-term effects of radiation exposure can include an increased risk of various types of cancer, particularly thyroid cancer, leukemia, and lung cancer. There can also be effects on the reproductive system, including sterility and potential impacts on future offspring.

One of the tragic legacies of the Chernobyl disaster was the widespread exposure to high levels of radiation, both among the emergency workers who responded to the accident and among the general population in the affected areas. The health effects of this radiation exposure continue to be a subject of ongoing research and monitoring.

Health Risks Faced by the People Exposed to Radiation

The Chernobyl disaster was a catastrophic event that exposed hundreds of thousands of people to high levels of ionizing radiation, both in the immediate aftermath and in the years that followed. These exposures have had profound and long-lasting health impacts.

In the immediate aftermath of the explosion, more than 600,000 liquidators—firefighters, soldiers, miners, and other workers—were brought in from all across the Soviet Union to fight fires, decontaminate the area, and build the sarcophagus around the damaged reactor. Many of these individuals received high doses of radiation, leading to acute radiation sickness in at least 134 cases. Acute radiation sickness can cause a range of symptoms, including nausea, vomiting, loss of appetite, severe headache, fever, fatigue, and weakness. In severe cases, it can lead to organ failure and death. At least 28 liquidators died in the first few months after the disaster from acute radiation sickness.

In the years following the disaster, an elevated risk of cancer, particularly thyroid cancer, has been observed among those exposed to the radiation. This increased risk has been most pronounced among those who were children at the time of the accident, due to the sensitivity of the developing thyroid gland to radiation. Many of these cancers were caused by radioactive iodine, which was released in large quantities during the explosion and was taken up by the thyroid gland when contaminated food and milk were consumed.

Another long-term health effect of the Chernobyl disaster has been an increase in the incidence of leukemia, a type of cancer that starts in the blood-forming cells of the bone marrow. This increase has been particularly notable among the liquidators, who received relatively high doses of radiation.

In addition to these specific diseases, many of those exposed to radiation from Chernobyl have suffered from a range of other health problems, including cardiovascular disease, cataracts, and various psychological and mental health issues. The stress and trauma of the disaster and its aftermath have had a significant impact on mental health, with increased rates of anxiety, depression, and post-traumatic stress disorder reported among those affected by the disaster.

There have also been concerns about the potential for genetic effects of the radiation exposure, leading to health problems in the children of those exposed. While there has been no clear evidence of a significant increase in birth defects or other genetic effects to date, this remains an area of ongoing research and monitoring.

The health risks faced by those exposed to radiation from the Chernobyl disaster highlight the devastating human cost of the disaster. They underscore the importance of robust safety measures and emergency preparedness in the operation of nuclear power plants, to prevent such a disaster from happening again.

OLIVER LANCASTER

Chapter 5: The Evacuation: Abandoning Pripyat

The Evacuation Process and Impact on the Affected Population

The scale and severity of the Chernobyl nuclear disaster necessitated a massive evacuation effort that displaced hundreds of thousands of people from their homes. This monumental task was undertaken in an atmosphere of fear, confusion, and misinformation, and it left a profound and lasting impact on the affected population.

In the immediate aftermath of the explosion, the Soviet government's first response was to try and downplay the severity of the incident. For the first 36 hours, life went on as usual for the residents of Pripyat, a city just a few kilometers from the Chernobyl power plant. Children went to school, parents went to work, and no one was aware of the deadly radioactive cloud that was enveloping their city.

On April 27, more than a day after the explosion, an evacuation order was finally issued. The residents of Pripyat were told to take only essential items as they were led to believe they would be away for just a few days. Buses were dispatched to transport the approximately 49,000 residents out of the city. In the subsequent weeks, the evacuation zone was expanded, eventually encompassing a 30-kilometer radius around the plant and resulting in the displacement of over 116,000 people.

The evacuation process, despite its urgent necessity, was marred by confusion and a lack of clear communication. Many of those being evacuated were not fully aware of the reasons for their sudden displacement, and rumors and fear spread quickly through the affected communities.

The impact of this evacuation on the affected population was significant and long-lasting. Those who were displaced from their homes lost not only their physical possessions but also their community and sense of place. Many suffered from 'Soviet Chernobyl syndrome', a term used to describe the psychological distress experienced by the survivors, marked by symptoms like anxiety, depression, and psychosomatic complaints.

Moreover, the evacuees faced stigma and discrimination in the places where they resettled, as fear and misinformation about radiation led to social isolation. Many struggled with unemployment and economic hardship, as they found it difficult to rebuild their lives in unfamiliar environments.

Children, who were the most vulnerable to the effects of radiation, faced unique challenges. Many were affected by health problems, particularly thyroid cancer, in the years following the disaster. The psychological impact on children was also significant, with many experiencing fear, confusion, and a sense of loss.

The long-term displacement of populations following the Chernobyl disaster also led to profound demographic changes in the affected areas. The once-bustling cities of Pripyat and Chernobyl have since turned into ghost towns, with buildings slowly being reclaimed by nature.

In retrospect, the evacuation process after the Chernobyl disaster and the subsequent impact on the displaced populations underline the long-term human and social costs of nuclear accidents. They highlight the necessity of adequate disaster preparedness, clear communication, and robust support systems for those affected by such events.

The Emotional and Psychological Toll on Evacuees

While the physical impact of the Chernobyl disaster is considerable and cannot be minimized, the emotional and psychological fallout among the evacuees and others affected by the disaster is equally compelling and heart-wrenching. From the immediate aftermath to the present day, the Chernobyl accident has caused widespread psychological distress, with profound implications for the mental health of those involved.

The initial phase of the disaster, marked by the sudden, unexpected evacuation and the fear of the unknown, brought immediate emotional and psychological turmoil. The evacuees, hastily relocated with only essential belongings and a promise of a temporary displacement, soon found their exile to be indefinite. This loss of home, possessions, community, and a sense of belonging in one swift stroke was a significant trauma.

The evacuees not only had to grapple with the displacement but also had to face the uncertainty and fear of radiation exposure. The invisible and insidious nature of radiation added a layer of terror and anxiety, contributing to an ongoing state of chronic stress. They had to live with the fear of developing radiation-induced illnesses, such as cancer, and the potential genetic effects on their future offspring.

Once evacuated, the resettlement process brought new challenges. Stigmatization became a significant issue, as relocated individuals and families were often viewed with fear and suspicion in their new communities due to the potential health risks associated with radiation exposure. This social isolation further exacerbated feelings of loneliness and dislocation.

Post-Traumatic Stress Disorder (PTSD) and other psychological disorders, including depression and anxiety, became prevalent among the evacuees. Many experienced recurring nightmares, insomnia, emotional numbness, and heightened irritability. Children, particularly, demonstrated regressive behaviors, academic difficulties, and psychological problems.

The term 'Chernobyl Syndrome' was coined to describe the combination of severe psychological and physical health problems experienced by the victims of the disaster. Notably, the chronic mental health issues often led to physical symptoms such as headaches, fatigue, and a general sense of poor health.

Moreover, the Soviet government's handling of the disaster, marked by secrecy and misinformation, led to a profound erosion of trust in authorities. This lack of trust further aggravated the psychological distress, leaving many individuals feeling helpless and forgotten.

It's important to remember that these psychological scars do not fade easily. Even decades after the disaster, many survivors continue to grapple with the psychological fallout. The disaster, indeed, continues to cast a long shadow on their lives.

The emotional and psychological toll of the Chernobyl disaster underscores the human aspect of such catastrophes. The implications extend far beyond the immediate disaster and physical health consequences, affecting the very fabric of people's lives and lasting long into the future.

OLIVER LANCASTER

Chapter 6: Battle Against the Unseen: Containing the Reactor

The Heroic Efforts of the Liquidators and Emergency Workers

In the immediate aftermath of the Chernobyl disaster, a group of men and women stepped forward to face the deadly challenge head-on. They were the liquidators, the emergency workers who were called upon to mitigate the disaster, often with little understanding of the danger they were facing. Their heroic efforts, in the face of extraordinary risks, represent a poignant chapter in the Chernobyl story.

The term 'liquidator' is derived from the Soviet policy of "liquidation" of the consequences of disasters. It refers to the civil and military personnel who were called in to deal with the immediate aftermath of the explosion. The number of liquidators is estimated to be around 600,000, although some sources suggest the number could be as high as 800,000. They included firefighters, soldiers, miners, engineers, nurses, and doctors from all across the Soviet Union.

From the outset, the liquidators faced an almost impossible task. The explosion had released an enormous amount of radioactivity, and the graphite moderator of the reactor was on fire, spreading radioactive smoke and dust into the atmosphere. The immediate priority was to put out the fires and prevent a thermal explosion that could have had even more catastrophic consequences.

Firefighters, who were among the first responders, entered a scene of unimaginable horror and chaos. Despite inadequate protective gear and little knowledge of the extreme radiation levels, they fought bravely to extinguish the flames. Many were exposed to lethal doses of radiation, and 28 of them died from acute radiation sickness in the following weeks.

Meanwhile, teams of miners were brought in to dig a tunnel under the reactor to create a cooling slab that would prevent a feared meltdown of the reactor into the earth, a scenario that could have contaminated the groundwater for thousands of kilometers. They worked in excruciatingly hot and cramped conditions, often not fully aware of the extent of the radiation danger.

Other liquidators were involved in the clean-up operations, which included tasks like decontamination, removal and burial of radioactive materials, and the construction of the sarcophagus to encase the damaged reactor. Many of them worked in shifts on the roof of the reactor, where radiation levels were so high that each worker could only spend a few minutes at a time.

The liquidators and emergency workers showed immense courage and resilience in their efforts to contain the disaster. Yet, their sacrifices were not without cost. Many suffered from severe health problems, including acute radiation sickness and an increased risk of cancer. The psychological toll was also immense, with many facing long-term mental health issues.

Despite the hardships and the toll on their health, many liquidators have expressed a sense of pride and duty in their work. They stepped into an unprecedented disaster, putting their lives on the line for the greater good. Their bravery and dedication, often overlooked in the grand narrative of the Chernobyl disaster, should not be forgotten.

The story of the liquidators serves as a poignant reminder of the human capacity for courage and resilience in the face of unimaginable adversity.

Techniques Used to Contain the Reactor and Prevent Further Damage

In the aftermath of the Chernobyl nuclear disaster, the imperative task at hand was to contain the damaged reactor and prevent further radioactive releases. The execution of this task demanded the deployment of diverse and complex techniques, a commitment to innovation in the face of adversity, and above all, the unflinching courage of those on the front lines.

Firstly, in the immediate aftermath of the explosion, emergency responders focused on extinguishing the fires and preventing a thermal explosion. Firefighters, despite their limited protective equipment, valiantly battled the flames in and around the reactor building. Meanwhile, a potential thermal explosion was averted through the swift action of liquidators and miners, who tunneled beneath the reactor to install a cooling slab and prevent the nuclear fuel from melting through the reactor floor and contaminating the groundwater.

Once the immediate threat of further explosions and fires was contained, attention turned to the daunting task of managing the radioactive materials within the reactor building. Helicopters were used to dump bags filled with sand, clay, lead, and boron onto the open reactor. These materials served a dual purpose. The sand and clay were intended to prevent further release of radioactive particles into the atmosphere, while the lead and boron were meant to absorb the radiation and slow down the ongoing nuclear reactions.

Following these aerial operations, the most ambitious and dangerous phase of the containment process began: the construction of the sarcophagus. Officially known as the "Shelter Structure," this was a massive steel and concrete structure designed to encase the damaged reactor and prevent the further release of radioactive material. Thousands of workers, often working in brief shifts due to the extreme radiation, were involved in this colossal construction project. Despite the hazardous conditions, the sarcophagus was completed in an astonishingly short period of six months.

The sarcophagus stood for almost 30 years, but with time, it began to show signs of wear and tear, posing a renewed risk of radioactive leakage. This led to the initiation of the New Safe Confinement project. This arch-shaped structure, large enough to encase the Notre Dame Cathedral, was constructed away from the site and then slid into place over the old sarcophagus in 2016. Its purpose is to provide a stable and secure containment of the reactor for at least the next 100 years, allowing for the eventual dismantling of the old sarcophagus and the safe removal of radioactive material.

Each of these containment measures was an engineering and logistical feat in its own right. Yet, behind every decision, behind every move, were the tireless and brave workers, who faced an invisible enemy and insurmountable odds. The techniques used in the containment of the Chernobyl reactor stand testament not only to human ingenuity but also to human bravery in the face of one of history's most daunting disasters.

OLIVER LANCASTER

Chapter 7: The Sarcophagus: Constructing a Shield

The Construction and Challenges of the Chernobyl Shelter or "Sarcophagus"

Following the initial containment efforts of the Chernobyl disaster, the most colossal and daring phase was the construction of a massive protective shell, known as the "sarcophagus" or officially, the Chernobyl Shelter. This edifice of steel and concrete was designed to contain the radioactive material within the damaged reactor. Its construction was a marvel of engineering prowess under extreme conditions, but it was not without its fair share of challenges.

After the immediate fires and the threat of a thermal explosion were under control, plans were drawn up to create a more permanent solution to contain the deadly radiation. The objective of the sarcophagus was to create a radiation-proof seal around the destroyed Reactor 4 and to stop further contamination into the environment.

The construction began in June 1986, just a few weeks after the explosion. Despite the urgency and the hazardous conditions, meticulous planning was required to ensure the structure's stability and effectiveness. The project employed about 400,000 workers, including engineers, construction workers, miners, and military personnel, known as liquidators.

The workers had to face high radiation levels, which made the construction process exceptionally challenging. Work shifts were kept to a bare minimum - often no longer than five minutes at a time - to limit exposure to the lethal radiation. Even then, the liquidators were exposed to high radiation doses, and many suffered from radiation sickness.

The sarcophagus was essentially a massive box of concrete walls and a steel roof, encasing the reactor and its lethal contents. It was about 165 meters long, 260 meters wide, and 110 meters tall. More than 400,000 cubic meters of concrete and 7,300 tons of metal framework were used in its construction. Due to the high radiation levels, much of the construction had to be done remotely, using cranes and robots. Despite the complexities, the sarcophagus was completed in just 206 days, an astounding feat given the circumstances.

However, the Chernobyl sarcophagus was far from a perfect solution. Built hastily in a high radiation environment, its structural integrity was a concern from the start. The sarcophagus wasn't sealed properly at the bottom, allowing for the continued contamination of groundwater. Also, it lacked a proper ventilation system, leading to corrosion and further structural instability over time.

Moreover, the sarcophagus was designed to last only about 30 years, with the expectation that a more permanent solution would be found in the meantime. As cracks began to appear in the structure and fears of collapse mounted, the international community funded the construction of a New Safe

Confinement, a massive, arch-shaped structure that was slid into place over the original sarcophagus in 2016.

The construction and the inherent challenges of the Chernobyl Shelter represent an important chapter in the story of human resilience, innovation, and cooperation in the face of unprecedented adversity.

The Sarcophagus: Purpose and Long-Term Implications

The purpose of the Chernobyl Shelter, or the "sarcophagus," was straightforward yet daunting: to contain the nuclear reactor's radioactive remnants and prevent further contamination of the environment. Yet, its existence and the subsequent developments that arose from its challenges have profound long-term implications in the realms of nuclear safety, international cooperation, and disaster management.

The immediate objective of the sarcophagus was to stem the flow of radioactive particles into the atmosphere from the destroyed reactor. Its immense structure, composed of concrete walls and a steel roof, was meant to act as a shield against radiation and contain the lethal contents within the damaged Reactor 4. In this primary role, despite its imperfections, the sarcophagus was largely successful.

The construction of the sarcophagus also had significant symbolic value, representing humanity's will to face and contain a disaster of unparalleled proportions. It was a monument to the bravery of the liquidators who built it, facing severe radiation hazards. The sarcophagus stands as a testament to human ingenuity and resilience under extreme conditions.

However, the long-term implications of the sarcophagus extend far beyond its immediate purpose. For one, it underscored the need for better safety measures in nuclear power generation. The disaster at Chernobyl and the subsequent challenges in containing the fallout served as a wakeup call to the world about the potential dangers of nuclear power if not adequately managed and regulated.

Moreover, the sarcophagus highlighted the limitations of unilateral efforts in managing nuclear disasters. Its design flaws and the subsequent need for a replacement underscored the importance of international collaboration in addressing such global threats. The construction of the New Safe Confinement was a shining example of international cooperation, with over 40 countries contributing to its funding and construction.

The long-term environmental implications of the sarcophagus are also significant. Even with the containment efforts, the surrounding area, known as the Exclusion Zone, remains heavily contaminated and will be uninhabitable for hundreds of years. This has spurred research into radioecology and the impact of radiation on wildlife and ecosystems, leading to new understandings and discoveries.

Furthermore, the sarcophagus and the broader Chernobyl disaster have had significant socio-political implications. The disaster exposed the flaws in the Soviet system's handling of the catastrophe, contributing to its ultimate dissolution. The continuing challenges related to the sarcophagus, such as worker safety, health issues, and resettlement of displaced populations, remain salient issues in Ukraine and Belarus.

The Chernobyl sarcophagus, in its function and legacy, is much more than a containment structure. It's a symbol of a human-made disaster and our response to it, a reminder of the power we wield and the responsibilities it entails. It is a lesson in humility, resilience, and the need for global cooperation in the face of shared threats.

OLIVER LANCASTER

Chapter 8: The Human Toll: Casualties and Health Consequences

Chapter 16: Examination of the Immediate and Long-Term Health Effects on the Affected Population

The Chernobyl disaster was an unprecedented event, causing a significant release of radioactive material that posed both immediate and long-term health hazards. Understanding these effects is critical to fully grasp the human toll of this nuclear catastrophe. The health impact was seen most profoundly among the emergency workers who responded to the crisis and the people living in the surrounding areas.

In the immediate aftermath, acute radiation sickness was the most prominent health issue faced by those exposed to high levels of radiation. This condition results from a large dose of radiation over a short period, and its severity depends on the amount of radiation absorbed by the body. The initial responders, including firefighters and workers at the power plant, faced lethal doses of radiation. Of these, 28 people died within a few weeks due to acute radiation sickness and thermal burns.

However, the more insidious effects of radiation are those that manifest over the long term. For the population living in and around the Chernobyl area, these effects have been profound and multi-faceted.

Perhaps the most well-documented long-term health effect is the dramatic increase in thyroid cancer cases among those who were children or adolescents at the time of the disaster. This rise in thyroid cancer is attributed to the high levels of radioactive iodine released during the accident. When inhaled or ingested through contaminated food or milk, the radioactive iodine is absorbed by the thyroid gland, leading to an increased risk of thyroid cancer. Fortunately, thyroid cancer is usually treatable when detected early, but the disease and its treatment can have significant impacts on quality of life.

Apart from thyroid cancer, there is also evidence of an increased incidence of leukemia and other hematological malignancies among cleanup workers and evacuees. There is ongoing research into the connection between radiation exposure and other types of cancers.

Radiation exposure is also linked to non-cancerous health effects. For example, studies have reported an increase in cardiovascular and cerebrovascular diseases among those exposed to radiation from the disaster. Furthermore, the impact of radiation on the immune system and the potential for genetic damage that can affect future generations is a critical area of research.

Beyond physical health, the disaster had a significant impact on mental health. The trauma of sudden evacuation, the fear of radiation and its potential effects, and the uncertainty about the future led to psychological and mental health issues, including depression, anxiety, and post-traumatic stress disorder. These effects have been observed among evacuees, cleanup workers, and those who continued to live in contaminated areas.

Moreover, the affected population has faced pervasive health-related stigma and discrimination, further exacerbating their mental health struggles. Many survivors have reported feeling 'tainted' by their association with the disaster, leading to social isolation and other psychosocial issues.

The health effects of the Chernobyl disaster are wide-ranging and enduring. The disaster highlights the importance of robust public health responses and long-term health monitoring following such incidents. It underscores the need for psychological support to disaster-affected populations and the importance of clear, accurate communication about the health risks of radiation to reduce fear and stigma.

The Rise of Cancer Cases and Other Radiation-Related Illnesses

The Chernobyl disaster caused an unprecedented release of radioactive particles into the environment, leading to significant exposure among those in the immediate vicinity and those involved in the cleanup efforts. This exposure had far-reaching health implications, most notably marked by a rise in cancer cases and other radiation-related illnesses.

The most pronounced increase in cancer following the disaster has been thyroid cancer among those who were children or adolescents at the time of the accident. The culprit was radioactive iodine, a byproduct of nuclear fission, released in large quantities during the reactor explosion. When ingested through contaminated air, food, or milk, radioactive iodine is absorbed by the thyroid gland. This resulted in a dramatic spike in thyroid cancer cases in the years following the disaster, particularly in Ukraine, Belarus, and parts of Russia. Fortunately, if detected early, thyroid cancer is treatable, but the treatment can have side effects and long-term health impacts.

However, the effects of radiation exposure from the Chernobyl disaster are not limited to thyroid cancer alone. Other types of cancer have also shown an increase, particularly among those who worked as liquidators and were directly exposed to high levels of radiation. Studies have reported a higher incidence of leukemia, particularly among cleanup workers and those living in the most contaminated areas. There is also evidence suggesting an increased risk of breast cancer and lung cancer among those exposed to Chernobyl's radiation.

In addition to cancers, other health conditions have been linked to the Chernobyl disaster. One notable health issue is the increased rate of cardiovascular disease. Research has shown that radiation exposure can damage blood vessels and heart tissue, leading to an increased risk of conditions such as coronary artery disease, strokes, and other circulatory system disorders.

Radiation sickness, a condition resulting from high levels of radiation exposure over a short period, was another immediate health impact of the disaster. Symptoms can range from nausea, fatigue, and loss of appetite to more severe effects such as damage to bone marrow and the cardiovascular system. In the most extreme cases, it can be fatal. Around 134 plant staff and emergency workers suffered from acute radiation sickness immediately after the disaster, with 28 people dying in the first few months due to this condition.

Lastly, it's important to note that radiation's impact on human health is not solely limited to physical ailments. The psychological toll of the disaster and its aftermath has been considerable. The fear of potential radiation effects, anxiety about health and the future, and the stress of displacement and upheaval have led to widespread mental health issues among survivors, including depression, anxiety, and post-traumatic stress disorder.

The full extent of the Chernobyl disaster's health impacts is still not entirely known, as radiation-related diseases can take decades to develop. Continued monitoring of the affected population and ongoing research into the health effects of radiation exposure is essential to fully understand and address the disaster's long-term health legacy.

Chapter 9: The Wildlife of Chernobyl: An Unexpected Resurgence

The Surprising Rebound of Nature and the Flourishing Ecosystem in the Exclusion Zone

In the wake of the Chernobyl disaster, an exclusion zone of about 2,600 square kilometers was created around the damaged reactor. This zone, uninhabited by humans, has become a somewhat surprising testament to nature's resilience and adaptability. Despite the high levels of radiation, the exclusion zone has transformed into a flourishing ecosystem, drawing the interest of scientists worldwide.

In the immediate aftermath of the disaster, the high levels of radiation had a noticeable effect on the area's flora and fauna. Pine forests near the reactor turned reddish-brown due to radiation damage, earning the nickname "Red Forest." Many animals in the vicinity of the reactor died or suffered from health problems due to radiation exposure.

However, over the years, the exclusion zone started to show signs of an unexpected revival. Devoid of human interference, nature began to reclaim the land. Forests grew over former farms, villages, and roads. Without the pressures of farming, hunting, and development, the animal population began to rebound.

Today, the Chernobyl Exclusion Zone almost resembles a wildlife preserve. Species not seen in the area for decades began to return. Wolves, bears, lynxes, bison, deer, and more than 200 species of birds have been documented in the zone. In a surprising turn of events, Przewalski's horses, which were endangered and introduced to the zone in the 90s as part of a conservation experiment, have thrived.

Even more intriguing is the adaptation of some species to the radioactive environment. Certain types of fungi, for instance, have been found to not only tolerate radiation but also to feed on it, a phenomenon known as radiosynthesis. Some birds have shown signs of adapting to the radiation, with changes in their antioxidant levels and the pigmentation of their plumage.

However, the thriving appearance of the exclusion zone does not mean radiation has had no effect on the wildlife. Studies have found evidence of genetic changes and damage in plants and animals, and some birds and insects have shown reduced populations. The long-term impacts of chronic radiation exposure on these populations remain a crucial area of research.

The recovery of the Chernobyl Exclusion Zone is a silver lining to a tragic event. The surprising rebound of nature offers a unique opportunity for scientists to study how ecosystems recover from disaster, adapt to change, and flourish in the absence of human interference. However, it is also a poignant reminder of the unforeseen consequences of human activity and the lasting legacy of nuclear disasters.

Impact of Radiation on Wildlife and Ongoing Studies

The Chernobyl Exclusion Zone, an area subjected to extreme radiation levels, has paradoxically become a flourishing wildlife refuge. While the ecosystem seems to thrive in the absence of human interference, radiation continues to impact the flora and fauna living within the zone. Ongoing studies aim to understand the extent of these effects, offering crucial insights into radiation biology and ecology.

While the ecosystem's apparent rebound is heartening, the picture is more complex under the surface. The impact of radiation varies among different species, with some appearing more resistant than others. The varying effects also depend on the organism's proximity to the damaged reactor, where radiation levels remain significantly higher.

Studies have shown genetic damage in several species in the zone. This damage manifests as mutations that can affect survival and reproduction rates. For instance, a study on the barn swallow, a common bird in the area, found higher rates of partial albinism, malformed feathers, and reduced survival rates compared to populations living outside the zone.

Insects, particularly those that rely on external sources of heat for survival, have also shown significant declines in population. Scientists attribute this to the fact that insects have a higher surface-area-to-volume ratio, which means they absorb more radiation.

On the other hand, larger mammals, such as wolves, deer, and boars, seem to be flourishing. The population of the Przewalski's horse, introduced to the zone in the 1990s, has grown, suggesting the species has adapted to the radiation levels. However, it's worth noting that their apparent success could be due more to the absence of human hunting and encroachment rather than an indication that radiation is harmless.

Perhaps one of the most fascinating developments is the emergence of so-called "radiotrophic fungi." These organisms appear to use melanin, the same pigment responsible for skin color in humans, to convert radiation into chemical energy for growth. The mechanism, though not yet fully understood, resembles photosynthesis, marking a fascinating example of adaptation to extreme conditions.

The Exclusion Zone has become a living laboratory for scientists studying radiation's long-term effects on living organisms and ecosystems. These studies are crucial in understanding the potential consequences of nuclear accidents and preparing for future incidents. Furthermore, this research helps us understand how life adapts to extreme environments, contributing to broader biological and ecological knowledge.

The story of wildlife in the Chernobyl Exclusion Zone is not simply one of doom or bloom. It's a complex narrative of resilience, adaptation, and the intricate ways nature responds to extreme conditions. It reminds us of the surprising resilience of life and the interplay between organisms and their environment, even in the face of human-made disasters.

64

Chapter 10: Investigating the Disaster: Lessons Learned

International Investigations and Findings Regarding the Chernobyl Disaster

The Chernobyl disaster marked a significant turning point in our understanding of nuclear safety. As the severity of the accident unfolded, international bodies quickly recognized the need to fully understand the sequence of events that led to the disaster, the immediate response, and the long-term implications. This led to several comprehensive investigations by international bodies, including the International Atomic Energy Agency (IAEA), the World Health Organization (WHO), and the United Nations Scientific Committee on the Effects of Atomic Radiation (UNSCEAR).

The IAEA, responsible for promoting peaceful use of nuclear energy and preventing its use for military purposes, led an international team of nuclear power experts in investigating the accident. Their findings were released in the 'INSAG-7' report in 1992, which replaced their initial 1986 report. The report highlighted the inherent design flaws of the RBMK-1000 reactors, particularly the positive void coefficient, which made them unstable at low power levels. The report also pointed to the absence of a robust containment structure, which led to the extensive release of radioactive materials into the environment.

While the design flaws were a significant factor, the IAEA also emphasized the role of human error. They pointed to the unsafe, unauthorized experiment conducted on the night of the disaster and the significant deviation from safety protocols. The plant operators, lacking a complete understanding of the reactor's physics, made crucial errors that contributed to the disaster.

The WHO, responsible for international public health, conducted extensive studies into the health effects of the Chernobyl disaster. They found a significant increase in thyroid cancers among those exposed to the fallout as children, a trend directly linked to the release of large amounts of radioactive iodine-131. Other reports indicated increased rates of other cancers and health issues among the cleanup workers and those living in highly contaminated areas.

UNSCEAR, which assesses radiation exposure and the environmental and human effects, has released several reports detailing the radiological consequences of the Chernobyl accident. These studies have provided an in-depth analysis of the release, dispersion, and deposition of radionuclides in the environment and the resultant exposure of humans and ecosystems.

The international investigations into the Chernobyl disaster have provided invaluable insights into nuclear safety, emergency response, and radiation's long-term effects on human health and the environment. The lessons learned from Chernobyl have influenced nuclear policy, reactor design, safety protocols, and emergency preparedness plans worldwide. They serve as a sobering reminder of the immense responsibility that comes with harnessing the power of the atom.

Key Lessons for Nuclear Safety and Disaster Management

The Chernobyl disaster forced the world to reevaluate the safety and management of nuclear power. In its aftermath, international investigations revealed critical shortcomings in reactor design, operational procedures, and emergency response. From these findings emerged essential lessons that have since shaped the approach to nuclear safety and disaster management.

Reactor Safety and Design: The disaster highlighted the need for inherently safe reactor designs. Design flaws in the RBMK-1000, such as its positive void coefficient and lack of a containment structure, played a critical role in the catastrophe. As a result, there has been a shift towards designs that prioritize 'passive' safety systems, which don't require human intervention or external power sources to mitigate a crisis. The disaster also led to significant improvements in the remaining RBMK reactors, with modifications made to reduce their inherent instability.

Operational Safety and Training: The role of human error in the Chernobyl disaster emphasized the importance of comprehensive training for plant operators. It's crucial that operators understand the intricacies of the reactor's physics and have clear guidelines for safe operation, including situations that deviate from normal operation. Furthermore, creating a culture of safety, where adherence to safety protocols is prioritized over operational targets, is fundamental.

Regulatory Oversight: Chernobyl underscored the importance of independent regulatory bodies that can provide stringent oversight of nuclear operations. These bodies must have the authority to enforce safety regulations and the ability to operate independently from pressures by the nuclear industry or government.

Emergency Preparedness and Response: The delayed evacuation of Pripyat following the disaster and the initial denial by Soviet authorities highlighted the need for robust emergency response plans. These plans must include guidelines for immediate actions, evacuation plans, and measures for limiting radiation exposure. Public communication in such situations is critical; authorities must provide accurate and timely information to the public to ensure their safety and maintain trust.

International Cooperation: The Chernobyl disaster transcended national borders, both in its immediate impacts and in the resulting cloud of radioactive fallout. This led to a renewed emphasis on international cooperation in nuclear safety. Information sharing and cooperation in safety standards, emergency planning, and response have been promoted through international agreements and organizations like the International Atomic Energy Agency.

A COMPREHENSIVE ACCOUNT OF THE NUCLEAR DISASTER

In the wake of Chernobyl, these lessons have been woven into the fabric of nuclear power operation and regulation, leading to considerable advancements in nuclear safety. However, the continued importance of these lessons cannot be overstated. As we continue to harness nuclear power, maintaining the highest standards of safety, preparedness, and oversight remains as vital as ever.

Chapter 11: Chernobyl's Legacy: The Exclusion Zone Today

Exploration of the Current State of the Exclusion Zone

Nearly four decades after the disaster, the Chernobyl Exclusion Zone remains one of the most unique areas on Earth. This 2,600-square-kilometer region, extending into Belarus, forms a silent testimony to one of humanity's most devastating technological disasters.

The zone is divided into two areas, each with varying degrees of access and contamination. The first is the 30-kilometer zone, which encircles the most heavily contaminated area, including the Chernobyl power plant itself. Then, there's the larger 10-kilometer zone, encapsulating the city of Pripyat and other nearby villages.

The Chernobyl nuclear power plant, now encased in the New Safe Confinement, is under constant monitoring. The Shelter Implementation Plan has ensured the safety of the damaged reactor, and ongoing efforts focus on managing the radioactive waste and eventually decommissioning the site.

Pripyat, once a bustling city home to the plant's workers and their families, now stands as a haunting monument of the past. Time seems to have frozen in the city, with its buildings, apartments, a Ferris wheel in the amusement park, and even children's toys lying abandoned and slowly being reclaimed by nature.

Interestingly, the Exclusion Zone has become a haven for wildlife, demonstrating nature's resilience in the face of disaster. The absence of humans has allowed many animal species to thrive, and the region has unintentionally become a unique wildlife reserve.

However, despite the return of wildlife, the area is far from safe for human habitation. The soil, water, and vegetation are still contaminated with various radionuclides, posing significant health risks. While radiation levels have decreased over time due to decay and weathering processes, some areas near the reactor still harbor dangerous levels of radiation.

In an unexpected turn of events, the Exclusion Zone has also become a tourist attraction in recent years. Guided tours allow visitors a glimpse into the ghostly world left behind by the disaster. Strict guidelines are in place to ensure the safety of these visitors, including prohibiting the touching of objects and consumption of food within the zone.

Ongoing scientific research in the area continues to provide invaluable data about the long-term impacts of radiation on the environment and ecosystems. The zone has become a unique laboratory for studying radiation's effects on wildlife and the environment.

The Chernobyl Exclusion Zone stands as a stark reminder of the catastrophic potential of nuclear power when not properly controlled. While its eerie beauty and surprising wildlife resurgence captivate the world, the lingering radiation underscores the lasting impact of the disaster.

Tourism and the Balance between Preservation and Safety

Tourism in the Chernobyl Exclusion Zone represents an unusual intersection of historical interest, dark tourism, and ecological observation. As the site of one of the most devastating nuclear accidents in history, it is both a grim reminder of a tragic past and an illustration of nature's unexpected resilience. However, this growing interest in Chernobyl tourism brings with it a challenging balance between preservation, safety, and responsible travel.

Safety is, of course, the primary concern in managing tourism in such a uniquely hazardous environment. The high radiation levels in certain areas pose a potential risk, so travel within the zone is strictly regulated by the Ukrainian government. Visitors are screened before entry and exit, are required to wear protective clothing, and must adhere to specific pathways and guidelines that minimize radiation exposure. Consumption of food or drink is not allowed inside the zone, and touching objects or structures is strictly forbidden.

In spite of these precautions, a certain level of risk remains, particularly in the case of illegal trespassing and unsupervised visits, which have been increasingly reported in recent years. The burgeoning fascination with the site, in part fueled by media and popular culture, has seen instances of 'stalkers' infiltrating the zone, often neglecting safety precautions, thus exposing themselves to significant health risks and disrupting the delicate ecology of the area.

Preservation of the zone, both as a testament to the disaster and as a unique ecological habitat, is another aspect of this balance. The relics of human habitation, such as the abandoned buildings in Pripyat, provide poignant reminders of the lives displaced by the disaster. They are historical landmarks bearing witness to a tragic event, slowly decaying and being reclaimed by nature.

Meanwhile, the burgeoning wildlife in the Exclusion Zone has made it a unique location for ecological studies. Preserving this unintended nature reserve and understanding how flora and fauna adapt to such an environment has become an important aspect of the Exclusion Zone's management.

Lastly, responsible tourism forms the crux of this balance. Visitors should be aware of the context and significance of the place they are visiting. The Exclusion Zone is not just a tourist attraction; it is a site of a tragic event that has caused immense suffering and continues to pose potential hazards. As such, it should be approached with the respect and seriousness it warrants.

The development of Chernobyl tourism, thus, lies in this challenging equilibrium between safety, preservation, and responsible travel. It offers a unique opportunity for educating the public about nuclear safety, the human cost of disaster, and the resilience of nature while ensuring the integrity and safety of the area are not compromised.

Chapter 12: Nuclear Energy After Chernobyl: Global Implications

The Impact of the Chernobyl Disaster on the Nuclear Power Industry Worldwide

The Chernobyl disaster sent shockwaves through the nuclear power industry and the global community at large. The event profoundly changed the world's perception of nuclear power and led to significant shifts in the industry's safety culture, technology, and policy.

First and foremost, Chernobyl led to a marked shift in safety culture. The disaster underscored the catastrophic potential of nuclear power if not properly controlled and highlighted the critical importance of safety over production. As a result, the industry saw a widespread push for increased safety standards, more rigorous operator training, and an overall emphasis on a culture of safety.

Technological changes also came in the aftermath of Chernobyl. The inherent design flaws of the RBMK-1000 reactor used at Chernobyl led to an increased emphasis on reactor design safety. This drove changes not just in new reactor designs, but also in the modification and upgrade of existing reactors worldwide. The industry has since moved towards designs with passive safety features that can automatically contain and mitigate accidents without relying on human intervention.

Regulatory oversight saw significant changes as well. The disaster showed the importance of having independent, robust regulatory bodies that could enforce safety regulations without the influence of industry or governmental pressures. In many countries, this led to a strengthening of regulatory agencies and the separation of regulatory and promotional functions.

The Chernobyl disaster also had a significant impact on nuclear policy both within and beyond the Soviet Union. The event fueled anti-nuclear sentiment and led many countries to reconsider their nuclear power programs. Some nations chose to scale back or terminate their plans for nuclear energy expansion, while others tightened regulations and increased safety measures. Germany, for instance, decided to phase out nuclear power entirely, a policy known as the "Energiewende" or energy transition.

Finally, the disaster highlighted the need for international cooperation and transparency. The cross-border impacts of the radioactive release and the initial secrecy of the Soviet Union underscored the importance of international coordination in nuclear safety, emergency preparedness, and response. This led to several international agreements and efforts to harmonize safety standards and foster a culture of openness and cooperation through international organizations like the International Atomic Energy Agency.

The Chernobyl disaster had a profound impact on the nuclear power industry. It was a stark wake-up call that triggered significant changes in safety culture, technology, regulatory oversight, policy, and international cooperation. Despite the enormous human cost and environmental damage, the lessons learned from Chernobyl have undoubtedly made nuclear power safer today.

Changes in Safety Regulations and Public Perception

In the aftermath of the Chernobyl disaster, there was a critical reassessment of nuclear safety regulations worldwide and a seismic shift in public perception towards nuclear power.

Safety Regulations:

Post-Chernobyl, the nuclear industry and regulatory bodies put a spotlight on safety. The disaster demonstrated that beyond the immediate vicinity of a nuclear accident, the international community could also be significantly affected, resulting in the push for harmonized safety standards across countries.

The International Atomic Energy Agency (IAEA) ramped up its efforts to develop a comprehensive body of safety standards and increase their application globally. A set of conventions was put in place, such as the Convention on Nuclear Safety, aimed at promoting a high level of nuclear safety worldwide through the enhancement of national measures and international cooperation.

Regulatory bodies worldwide became more stringent and rigorous. There was a general trend toward strengthening regulatory independence to ensure that the safety mission was not compromised by other interests. Regulatory bodies expanded their focus to include a plant's safety culture, not just its technical compliance.

Safety protocols were revised to include severe, beyond-design-basis accidents. The concept of 'defence in depth' was reinforced. This strategy involves creating multiple independent and redundant layers of safety measures and barriers to prevent the release of radioactive materials.

The importance of emergency preparedness and response was emphasized, leading to improved national and international systems for managing emergency situations and protecting the public. Regulatory frameworks for managing nuclear and radiological emergencies were strengthened.

Public Perception:

The public perception of nuclear power underwent a dramatic change after the Chernobyl disaster. The accident struck a critical blow to the public's confidence in nuclear energy, particularly in Europe, turning public opinion in many countries against nuclear power.

The perception of nuclear power as a dangerous source of energy increased significantly. Public concerns over the safety of nuclear power plants and the potential long-term health effects of radiation were heightened.

A COMPREHENSIVE ACCOUNT OF THE NUCLEAR DISASTER

Fear and distrust led to powerful anti-nuclear movements in several countries, culminating in large public demonstrations. The political impact of this shift in public opinion was significant. Some countries like Italy and Germany decided to phase out nuclear power. In others, the development of new nuclear power plants was halted, or plans for expansion were significantly curtailed.

Even today, public opinion on nuclear energy remains polarized. While some see it as a necessary part of the solution to climate change due to its low greenhouse gas emissions, others remain wary due to the potential risks involved and the issue of nuclear waste disposal.

In essence, the Chernobyl disaster prompted a new era of nuclear safety and left a lasting imprint on public perception. It taught the world a harsh lesson about the importance of safety and the potential consequences when it is not prioritized.

OLIVER LANCASTER

Chapter 13: Pripyat: A Ghost Town Frozen in Time

A Detailed Exploration of the Abandoned City of Pripyat

To truly grasp the impact of the Chernobyl disaster, one must journey to the heart of the Exclusion Zone, where the abandoned city of Pripyat lies. Once a thriving city and the symbol of Soviet progress, Pripyat now stands as a poignant testament to the scale of the disaster, a silent city frozen in time.

A Brief History:

Pripyat was founded on February 4, 1970, as the ninth nuclear city (a type of closed city) in the Soviet Union, to serve the nearby Chernobyl Nuclear Power Plant. The city was officially proclaimed in 1979 and became the home of the plant's employees and their families, housing a population of almost 50,000 people.

The Heart of Pripyat:

At the city's core lies Lenin Square, once teeming with life and activity. Dominating the square is the impressive Polissya hotel, where the plant's guests stayed, and from where helicopters coordinated the initial response to the disaster. On the opposite side, the towering building of Energetik, a cultural palace, hosted numerous recreational activities including concerts, boxing matches, and dance classes.

The Ghost Town:

As you wander through the city, the streets echo with silence, broken only by the rustling wind. Trees sprout from the cracked pavement, and nature gradually reclaims the urban landscape. The sight of dilapidated apartment blocks, with their broken windows and balconies taken over by flora, paints a haunting image of life abruptly halted.

Eerie Reminders:

Perhaps the most famous symbol of the city's abrupt end is the amusement park with its rusting Ferris wheel, scheduled to open on May 1, 1986, just days after the disaster. The sight of the untouched bumper cars and the motionless Ferris wheel is particularly eerie, a stark contrast to the joy they were meant to inspire.

Pripyat's schoolrooms and kindergartens are some of the most disturbing sights. Children's dolls, textbooks, and drawings are scattered, left behind in the hurried evacuation. These rooms offer a stark reminder of the human toll of the disaster.

Nature's Return:

Amidst the decay, life finds a way. Nature has started to reclaim the city, with flora covering buildings and fauna returning to the area. Despite the harsh circumstances, Pripyat has inadvertently become a nature reserve.

The Future:

Despite the radiation, Pripyat has drawn the attention of scientists, historians, and even tourists. It offers a unique snapshot of Soviet life frozen in time and a stark reminder of the consequences of nuclear disaster.

Pripyat is more than an abandoned city; it's a haunting symbol of human tragedy, a monument to the tens of thousands who lost their homes, and a testament to nature's resilience in the face of disaster.

Personal Accounts of Life Before and After the Disaster

To understand the full human impact of the Chernobyl disaster, we must turn to the personal accounts of those whose lives were forever altered by the events of April 26, 1986. The voices of Pripyat's former residents paint a vivid picture of life before and after the disaster.

Life Before the Disaster:

Prior to the disaster, Pripyat was viewed as a model city and a place of opportunity. Designed for the workers of the Chernobyl Nuclear Power Plant and their families, it boasted modern amenities that were considered luxurious for the time. A school teacher, Valentina, remembers: "We had everything - schools, kindergartens, shops, a cultural center, and a cinema. It was a wonderful, vibrant place to live. Our children were happy."

Vladimir, a former engineer at the plant, recalls the sense of purpose and pride associated with working at Chernobyl. "We were contributing to the power and development of our nation," he says. "Working at the plant was considered prestigious. We were a close-knit community."

The Day of the Disaster:

Many recount the confusion and fear that surrounded the day of the disaster. Despite the explosion that rocked the plant, many residents were not immediately aware of the severity of the situation. As Anna, a former resident, recollects, "The day was beautiful, sunny. There was no panic, just confusion. It was only later that we understood something terrible had happened."

The Aftermath:

Accounts of the evacuation on April 27th echo with a sense of disbelief and heartbreak. Residents were given just a few hours to gather their belongings and were assured they would return in a few days. But this was not to be. For Lyudmila, a former nurse, leaving her home was one of the hardest moments of her life. "We left everything, thinking we would be back soon. We didn't know we were saying goodbye to our lives as we knew them."

Life After Chernobyl:

Life after the disaster was marked by displacement, health problems, and psychological trauma. Many survivors struggled with the stigma associated with being a 'Chernobyl victim'. The survivors faced significant health risks from radiation exposure, with many developing cancer or other radiation-related diseases years later. The psychological toll was also immense. Anxiety, depression, and PTSD were prevalent among survivors.

Despite the hardships, the former residents of Pripyat remember their city with a sense of longing. "We lost our home," says Igor, a former power plant worker. "But more than that, we lost our community, our friends, our sense of belonging. Chernobyl took that from us."

These personal stories serve as a poignant reminder that behind the global discussions of nuclear power and safety, behind the statistics and the science, are the people who lived through the disaster - people whose lives were irrevocably altered by the events of that fateful April night.

OLIVER LANCASTER

Chapter 14: Voices from Chernobyl: Testimonies and Personal Stories

Compilation of Personal Accounts from Survivors, Liquidators, and Residents

The Chernobyl disaster is a story of loss, sacrifice, and resilience told best by the voices of those who lived through it. Here we share a collection of personal accounts from survivors, liquidators, and residents, each shedding light on a different aspect of the tragedy.

Survivors:

Anatoly, a former plant worker recalls the night of the explosion: "I remember a tremendous sound and a wave of pressure that knocked me off my feet. I looked towards the reactor and saw a ball of fire. It was a sight I'll never forget."

Tatiana, a resident of Pripyat, shares her evacuation experience: "We were told to pack a suitcase and take our documents. We thought we were leaving for just a few days. If I knew I would never return, I would have looked at my home, my city, a little longer."

Liquidators:

Vasily, a firefighter, was one of the first responders: "We were told it was a roof fire. We had no idea about the radiation.

We fought the fire without any protective gear. Many of my comrades started to vomit and collapse after a few hours."

Sergey, a military liquidator, recounts the cleanup efforts: "We worked in shifts, shoveling the radioactive debris. We were given vodka and told it would help against the radiation. Many of my friends from those days are not alive anymore."

Residents:

Marina, a child during the disaster, remembers the confusing days after the explosion: "I remember the beautiful red fire truck that stood in front of our building. But my parents didn't let me play outside. I didn't understand why."

Alexander, who lived in a nearby village, talks about life post-disaster: "We were relocated to a different part of Ukraine. But it wasn't home. Our health worsened over the years, and there was this constant fear of radiation."

Elena, a resident of Pripyat, shares her longing for her lost city: "Our life in Pripyat was good. We had everything we needed, and we were happy. Now, all that's left are memories and an unbearable longing for what we've lost."

Each of these stories provides a small glimpse into the vast human tragedy that was the Chernobyl disaster. They tell a tale of a promising city abruptly silenced, a people forever marked by an invisible enemy, and a world grappling with the consequences of a nuclear nightmare.

Emotional Experiences and Their Impact

on Individuals and Communities

The Chernobyl disaster did not merely cause physical devastation; it left deep emotional scars on individuals and communities. The magnitude of the disaster, the loss of home and community, the long-term health concerns, and the social stigma associated with being a "Chernobyl victim" all contributed to significant emotional distress.

Individual Impact:

On an individual level, the emotional fallout was vast and varied. The initial reactions ranged from disbelief and shock to fear and panic. The sudden, forced evacuation without a chance for a proper goodbye induced a profound sense of loss. Many survivors experienced feelings of homesickness and nostalgia for their old life.

The disaster also instilled a perpetual state of fear and uncertainty. Worries about the unseen threat of radiation and its potential impact on personal health and the health of loved ones became a persistent stressor. The high rates of cancer and other illnesses among the survivors only intensified these fears.

Survivors also faced stigmatization and discrimination, leading to feelings of isolation. Many reported being treated as 'contaminated' or 'infectious,' creating a sense of shame and exacerbating feelings of loss and dislocation.

Moreover, the significant number of deaths and illnesses among survivors led to widespread experiences of grief. Additionally, many survivors suffered from post-traumatic stress disorder (PTSD), characterized by intrusive memories of the disaster, heightened anxiety, and avoidance of reminders of the traumatic event.

Community Impact:

The disaster had a profound impact on the community fabric of the affected regions. The forced evacuation and displacement resulted in the dissolution of close-knit communities, leading to a collective sense of loss. Communities were fragmented, and social networks were disrupted, which often resulted in a lack of social support and increased feelings of loneliness and isolation.

The stigma associated with the Chernobyl disaster also had a significant impact on community dynamics. There was often mistrust and resentment between the relocated communities and the local population, further hindering social integration and creating tension in the newly formed communities.

The sense of unity and shared experience in the face of disaster also emerged as a significant aspect of the community's emotional experience. Many survivors expressed feelings of kinship and solidarity with their fellow survivors, and the disaster spurred acts of communal support and camaraderie.

The emotional experiences following the Chernobyl disaster were as significant and enduring as the physical consequences. The disaster left a lasting imprint on the emotional landscape of the survivors and the affected communities, shaping their experiences and responses in the years that followed.

A COMPREHENSIVE ACCOUNT OF THE NUCLEAR DISASTER

Chapter 15: The Chernobyl Nuclear Disaster in Popular Culture

Examination of the Representation of Chernobyl in Literature, Film, and Art

The Chernobyl disaster has deeply permeated the world of literature, film, and art, serving as a symbol of human folly, technological hubris, and environmental catastrophe. Each medium provides a unique lens through which to view and understand the disaster and its lasting repercussions.

Literature:

Literary responses to Chernobyl are diverse, reflecting the myriad of human experiences and emotions it engendered. Perhaps the most influential work is Svetlana Alexievich's "Voices from Chernobyl." This collection of personal testimonies brings to life the human tragedies and heroism behind the disaster, illuminating the psychological and social impacts of the event.

There are also numerous memoirs and diaries that provide first-hand accounts of the disaster. These works capture the immediacy of the event and its aftermath, offering intimate insights into the experiences of survivors, liquidators, and those involved in the disaster response.

Film and Television:

Film and television have played a significant role in shaping public understanding and perception of Chernobyl. The 2019 miniseries "Chernobyl" by HBO portrayed the disaster and the Soviet government's response in visceral detail, highlighting both the scientific and political aspects of the catastrophe.

Documentaries like "The Battle of Chernobyl" provide factual accounts of the disaster, exploring the causes, immediate response, and the long-term effects of the radiation. Other films, like "Chernobyl Diaries," use the disaster as a backdrop for horror narratives, reflecting the cultural association of Chernobyl with fear and contamination.

Art:

Artists across different mediums have been drawn to Chernobyl, using the disaster and its aftermath as powerful sources of inspiration. Photography has been particularly impactful in depicting the eeriness of the Exclusion Zone and the abandoned city of Pripyat. Haunting images of deserted schools, crumbling buildings, and the notorious Ferris wheel encapsulate the stark reality of a life abruptly abandoned.

Paintings and installations often grapple with themes of loss, memory, and the intersection of technology and nature. Some artists use radioactive materials or incorporate radiation measurements into their works, creating a tangible link to the disaster.

The representation of Chernobyl in literature, film, and art serves as a collective attempt to comprehend and express the complex realities and emotional resonances of the disaster. These cultural reflections continue to ensure the disaster's enduring place in our global consciousness.

Cultural Impact and the Dissemination of Information

The cultural impact of the Chernobyl disaster is pervasive, extending beyond the borders of the Soviet Union to penetrate global consciousness. The disaster has come to symbolize the potential dangers of nuclear power, influencing public perception and policy worldwide.

Cultural Impact:

Chernobyl, as a cultural event, was a defining moment of the late 20th century. It marked a turning point in our understanding of nuclear power and its risks, causing a significant shift in the public's trust in this technology. It also highlighted the potential consequences of bureaucratic opacity and negligence in the face of such high-stakes technology.

Chernobyl is also deeply entrenched in popular culture, being referenced in films, television shows, books, music, and video games. These portrayals, while varying in their historical accuracy, contribute to the collective understanding and memory of the event. They present the disaster as a warning of the potential consequences of unchecked technological progress and the destructive potential of human error.

Dissemination of Information:

The dissemination of information about the Chernobyl disaster played a critical role in shaping its cultural impact. The initial secrecy surrounding the disaster by the Soviet government sparked international outrage and suspicion, leading to long-term mistrust and fear.

The media's role in disseminating information about the disaster and its aftermath has been essential. While initial coverage was marked by uncertainty and misinformation due to the Soviet government's secrecy, media outlets worldwide played a vital role in revealing the true extent of the disaster and its far-reaching consequences.

The advent of the internet has also been crucial in facilitating access to information about the disaster. Countless articles, documentaries, photographs, survivor testimonies, and academic studies are readily accessible, ensuring that the history and lessons of Chernobyl continue to be available to the global audience.

Scientific and academic research on Chernobyl has been instrumental in deepening our understanding of the disaster. Numerous studies have been conducted on the health effects of radiation, the environmental impact, the efficacy of containment efforts, and the psychological effects on survivors and their descendants.

The cultural impact of Chernobyl and the dissemination of information about the disaster are deeply intertwined. They have collectively shaped the narrative of Chernobyl, influencing our perception and understanding of nuclear power and its potential hazards.

OLIVER LANCASTER

Chapter 16: Chernobyl Today: Scientific Research and Monitoring

———

Ongoing Scientific Studies and Research on the Effects of the Disaster

Three decades after the Chernobyl disaster, scientific research into its effects continues to evolve, providing valuable insights into the long-term consequences of nuclear accidents. These studies span several disciplines, from medicine and epidemiology to ecology and radiation physics.

Health Studies:

Health studies form a crucial part of ongoing research. The primary focus has been on the risk of thyroid cancer due to exposure to radioactive iodine, particularly in those who were children or adolescents at the time of the disaster. The World Health Organization (WHO) has confirmed a significant increase in thyroid cancers among this group.

Research has also focused on the potential link between radiation exposure and other types of cancer, such as leukemia and breast cancer. Though findings have been less definitive due to factors like the latency period of cancers, the aging population, and other health risk factors.

Studies are also being conducted on the mental health effects of the disaster, including post-traumatic stress disorder, depression, and anxiety. The prolonged displacement, fear of radiation, and the social stigma have had significant psychological impacts on survivors and their descendants.

Ecological and Environmental Studies:

The disaster has inadvertently created a living laboratory for studying the effects of radiation on the environment. Scientists continue to monitor the Chernobyl Exclusion Zone, observing the resilience and recovery of ecosystems and studying the genetic and physiological effects of radiation on plants and animals.

Interestingly, the absence of humans has led to a significant rebound of wildlife in the Exclusion Zone, with populations of wolves, deer, and other wildlife thriving. However, studies have found genetic mutations and other physiological changes in some organisms, indicating the ongoing impact of radiation.

Radiological Studies:

Ongoing research is also being conducted on the radiological conditions in the Exclusion Zone, including studies on the spread and behavior of radionuclides, their penetration into soils and water systems, and their bioaccumulation in the food chain.

The Chernobyl Shelter, built to contain the damaged reactor, is also an area of ongoing research. Studies are being conducted to monitor the structural integrity of the shelter and the status of the radioactive material inside.

Ongoing scientific studies and research on the effects of the Chernobyl disaster continue to provide valuable insights into the long-term consequences of nuclear accidents. They underscore the need for vigilance, preparedness, and a deep understanding of the potential risks associated with nuclear power.

Environmental Monitoring and the Future Outlook

The aftermath of the Chernobyl disaster has necessitated a continuous and rigorous environmental monitoring program. The monitoring efforts and the resulting data inform policies for managing the affected area, provide insights into long-term radiation effects, and guide future response strategies for nuclear accidents.

Environmental Monitoring:

The environmental monitoring of the Chernobyl Exclusion Zone involves measuring the levels of radiation and the presence of radionuclides in air, soil, water, and biota. A comprehensive network of radiation monitoring stations has been installed in the area to continuously track changes in radiation levels.

Studies are also being conducted to monitor the contamination levels in the food and water supply and the potential for bioaccumulation of radionuclides in the food chain. In particular, scientists are monitoring the presence of

Cesium-137, Strontium-90, and Plutonium isotopes, which pose long-term environmental risks due to their long half-lives.

Flora and fauna within the Exclusion Zone are also continuously monitored. Despite the high radiation levels, the zone has witnessed a surge in biodiversity, becoming a de facto nature reserve. However, the impact of radiation on the health and genetics of these populations is an area of ongoing study.

Future Outlook:

Despite the grim history of Chernobyl, the future of the Exclusion Zone offers intriguing possibilities. The area has become a focal point for research on nuclear accidents' long-term environmental effects, yielding invaluable scientific data. The rapid rebound of nature in the Exclusion Zone also provides unique opportunities for studying the ecological processes that unfold when human pressure is removed from the environment.

The New Safe Confinement structure built over the initial sarcophagus is designed to last 100 years, during which the remaining nuclear fuel will be extracted and safely disposed of. Scientists and engineers will continue to monitor the stability of the structure and the conditions inside the shelter to ensure there are no further leaks of radiation.

Furthermore, the Exclusion Zone has seen a rise in controlled tourism, providing a source of income for the region and serving as a stark reminder of the disaster's repercussions. While there are concerns about safety and the risk of glorifying a site of tragedy, managed access ensures that the lessons of Chernobyl remain a part of global memory.

The Chernobyl disaster has underscored the importance of rigorous environmental monitoring in the aftermath of nuclear accidents. The future outlook for the area, while still challenging, provides unique opportunities for research, conservation, and remembrance.

Chapter 17: Nuclear Disasters Post-Chernobyl: Lessons Applied

Comparison with Other Nuclear Accidents: Three Mile Island and Fukushima

Chernobyl, Three Mile Island, and Fukushima Daiichi are three of the most significant nuclear accidents in history. Each incident presents unique circumstances, technical failures, and response strategies, but they all share the common theme of dire consequences for human health and the environment. A comparison of these incidents provides valuable lessons on nuclear safety, crisis management, and the long-term impacts of such accidents.

Three Mile Island:

The Three Mile Island accident occurred on March 28, 1979, in Pennsylvania, United States. A cooling malfunction in the plant's second reactor led to a partial meltdown. However, unlike Chernobyl, there was no full reactor explosion or severe radioactive fire.

The containment structure of the Three Mile Island reactor held up and prevented the majority of the radioactive material from entering the environment. Therefore, the amount of radiation released into the atmosphere was significantly less than Chernobyl.

The Three Mile Island incident led to sweeping changes in the regulation and operation of nuclear plants in the United States. It demonstrated the importance of clear communication protocols during a crisis and underscored the need for robust safety measures and regular training and drills for nuclear plant workers.

Fukushima Daiichi:

The Fukushima Daiichi nuclear disaster occurred on March 11, 2011, in Japan, triggered by a massive earthquake and subsequent tsunami. The power supply and cooling functions of three reactors were compromised, leading to nuclear meltdowns and releases of radioactive materials.

The Fukushima disaster, like Chernobyl, involved a significant release of radioactive materials, necessitating the evacuation of residents in a 20 km radius. However, the containment structures, although damaged, managed to prevent a larger-scale disaster.

Fukushima highlighted the vulnerability of nuclear power plants to natural disasters and the importance of incorporating such considerations into plant design and safety protocols. It also drew attention to the necessity of prompt and transparent communication in the wake of a nuclear accident.

Common Lessons:

While each disaster—Chernobyl, Three Mile Island, and Fukushima—occurred under different circumstances and involved different types of reactors and failures, they collectively highlight several critical lessons. These include the need for rigorous safety measures, continuous staff training, thorough emergency preparedness plans, robust plant design, transparent communication, and timely evacuation procedures.

Despite the tragic consequences, these incidents have led to significant improvements in nuclear safety standards worldwide, with countries revising their regulations and safety protocols to prevent similar disasters in the future.

Safety Improvements and Precautions Implemented Globally

The Chernobyl disaster and other major nuclear incidents have indelibly shaped the approach to nuclear safety worldwide. They have led to a greater understanding of potential hazards and spurred the implementation of extensive safety improvements and precautions in nuclear facilities across the globe.

Design and Construction:

The lessons learned from Chernobyl have significantly influenced the design and construction of nuclear power plants. The RBMK reactors' inherent design flaws that contributed to the Chernobyl disaster are now widely studied to ensure such design errors are not repeated. Modern reactors are built with multiple redundant and diverse safety systems to prevent the possibility of catastrophic accidents.

The containment structures, which prevent the release of radioactive materials into the environment in case of an accident, have also been improved. For example, the design used in Western nuclear power plants, which proved successful during the Three Mile Island accident, has been adopted widely.

Safety Protocols and Operational Management:

Operational procedures and safety protocols have been thoroughly revised post-Chernobyl. Nuclear plants now operate under a "safety culture," where the emphasis is on rigorous adherence to safety procedures, constant vigilance, and a proactive approach to identify and rectify potential safety issues.

There's a greater emphasis on worker training, ensuring all staff understand the reactors' workings and are capable of responding effectively to any emergency. "Safety culture" training encourages workers to prioritize safety over operational considerations and encourages them to voice any safety concerns without fear of reprisal.

Regulation and Oversight:

The oversight and regulation of nuclear power have also been enhanced. Domestic nuclear regulatory bodies have tightened their regulations and increased their scrutiny of nuclear power plants. Internationally, the role of the International Atomic Energy Agency (IAEA) has been strengthened, with increased cross-border cooperation to improve nuclear safety globally.

Emergency Preparedness:

Post-Chernobyl, there's been a greater focus on emergency preparedness. Detailed and realistic emergency response plans are now mandatory for all nuclear facilities. These plans are regularly tested through drills involving plant personnel, emergency services, and sometimes even the local population.

Transparency and Communication:

Chernobyl highlighted the devastating consequences of misinformation and lack of transparency in the face of a nuclear accident. As a result, there is now a stronger focus on open communication and public transparency during nuclear incidents. The IAEA's Incident and Emergency Centre, established in the wake of Chernobyl, provides a communication platform to share critical information during a nuclear or radiological emergency.

The safety improvements and precautions implemented post-Chernobyl reflect an industry-wide commitment to ensuring that such a disaster does not recur. However, the quest for absolute safety in nuclear energy generation is ongoing, with continuous efforts to learn, adapt, and improve safety measures.

Chapter 18: Chernobyl's Long-Term Consequences: The Road to Recovery

Efforts to Rebuild and Rehabilitate Affected Areas

In the aftermath of the Chernobyl disaster, the Soviet government was confronted with a monumental task: the rehabilitation and rebuilding of the affected areas, relocation and support of displaced populations, and managing the ongoing radiological risks. Despite the magnitude of the disaster, significant efforts have been undertaken over the past decades to restore a sense of normalcy to the affected regions.

Evacuation and Resettlement:

In the immediate aftermath of the disaster, over 116,000 people were evacuated from the area surrounding the Chernobyl power plant. In subsequent years, the evacuation zone was expanded, and an additional 230,000 people were relocated. The government provided these displaced persons with new homes and attempted to help them rebuild their lives, though many continued to face difficulties due to social stigma and health issues.

Decontamination and Rehabilitation:

A massive decontamination effort was undertaken to reduce the radiation levels in the affected areas. This involved removing and disposing of topsoil, washing down buildings and roads, and applying chemicals to the soil to prevent the uptake of radionuclides by plants. While it was not possible to restore the most heavily contaminated areas to their original state, these efforts succeeded in reducing radiation levels significantly in many regions.

The government also undertook extensive efforts to rehabilitate the affected areas economically and socially. This included providing medical services, creating new jobs to replace those lost due to the disaster, and offering social support to the affected communities.

The Exclusion Zone Today:

Today, the Chernobyl Exclusion Zone, which covers an area of approximately 2,600 square kilometers, remains largely uninhabited by humans. However, it is far from being a wasteland. The area has been transformed into a unique sanctuary for wildlife, and extensive efforts are being made to study and preserve this unique ecosystem.

There has also been a focus on harnessing the economic potential of the Exclusion Zone. In recent years, there has been a surge in tourism to the area, with visitors drawn by the eerily preserved ghost towns and the fascinating (if grim) history of the place. This has brought much-needed income to the region and has helped to raise awareness about the disaster and its consequences.

Future Outlook:

Looking to the future, efforts continue to monitor and contain the lingering radiation risks, provide ongoing support to the affected populations, and manage the ecological, economic, and social challenges in the Exclusion Zone. The disaster's long-term impact continues to unfold, but the resilience of the affected communities and the surprising recovery of nature offer a glimmer of hope in the face of adversity.

The efforts to rebuild and rehabilitate the areas affected by the Chernobyl disaster represent a testament to human resilience in the face of tragedy. The ongoing challenges serve as a poignant reminder of the long-lasting consequences of nuclear disasters and the importance of preventing such incidents in the future.

Socio-Economic Challenges and the Importance of Community Support

The aftermath of the Chernobyl disaster was not just a story of radioactive fallout and health crises. It was also a tale of disrupted livelihoods, social stigma, and long-lasting socio-economic challenges. The catastrophe highlighted the integral role of community support in addressing these multifaceted issues.

Socio-Economic Challenges:

The immediate evacuation and subsequent resettlement affected more than 350,000 people, uprooting them from their homes and causing significant upheaval. These people faced the daunting task of rebuilding their lives in unfamiliar locations. The loss of jobs, homes, and community ties was further compounded by the enduring health concerns stemming from radiation exposure.

The evacuation also resulted in a significant economic decline in the region. Agriculture, which had been the mainstay of the local economy, was deeply impacted due to the contamination of farmland. The closing down of the Chernobyl plant itself also led to job losses, further exacerbating the economic hardship.

The Importance of Community Support:

In the face of such overwhelming adversity, community support proved to be a vital lifeline. This support took various forms, from governmental assistance to grassroots community initiatives and international aid.

Government programs were launched to support the displaced people, providing housing and financial assistance, healthcare services, and initiatives to create job opportunities in the new settlements. Despite criticism over the handling of the immediate aftermath of the disaster, these programs were essential in providing a foundation for the affected individuals to rebuild their lives.

Grassroots community initiatives also played a critical role. Local non-profit organizations and volunteer groups stepped in to fill the gaps in the state support system. They provided much-needed services such as counseling, healthcare, and educational programs about radiation safety. They also worked to foster a sense of community among the displaced people, helping to alleviate the psychological impact of the disaster.

The international community also pitched in, with international organizations and foreign governments providing aid and technical assistance. This global support was instrumental in many of the major projects, such as the construction of the New Safe Confinement structure.

The Way Forward:

The socio-economic challenges posed by the Chernobyl disaster underscore the need for comprehensive disaster response strategies that go beyond immediate containment and cleanup efforts. It is crucial to consider the long-term socio-economic impacts and to provide ongoing support to affected communities.

Looking ahead, community support remains a critical component in addressing these challenges. Whether it is in the form of government programs, local initiatives, or international aid, such support can make a significant difference in helping affected communities recover and rebuild in the wake of a disaster.

OLIVER LANCASTER

Chapter 19: Remembering Chernobyl: Commemorations and Remembrance

Memorialization and Commemorative Events Honoring the Victims

In the years following the Chernobyl disaster, various memorialization efforts and commemorative events have been established to honor the victims and remember the lessons learned. These acts of remembrance serve not only as a tribute to those who suffered and lost their lives, but also as a powerful reminder of the cost of negligence and the importance of vigilance in the management of nuclear power.

Memorial Sites and Monuments:

Several memorial sites and monuments have been erected in Ukraine, Belarus, and Russia in memory of the Chernobyl victims. Perhaps the most well-known is the monument "To Those Who Saved the World," located in Chernobyl town. This monument is dedicated to the firefighters, liquidators, and other emergency workers who risked their lives in the immediate aftermath of the explosion.

In Slavutych, the city built to house the evacuated Chernobyl power plant workers and their families, a memorial park contains stone plaques dedicated to the

villages abandoned due to contamination. The monument is a poignant reminder of the human displacement caused by the disaster.

Similarly, in the city of Kiev, the "Chernobyl Victims' Memorial" pays homage to the heroism of those who sacrificed their lives to combat the nuclear disaster and commemorates those who suffered as a result.

Commemorative Events:

Every year on April 26, numerous events are held to mark the anniversary of the Chernobyl disaster. These range from solemn ceremonies and candlelight vigils to exhibitions, film screenings, and academic conferences.

During these events, people gather at memorial sites to lay flowers and light candles in honor of those who lost their lives. Prayers and moments of silence are held, and often, the names of the deceased are read out loud.

In recent years, these commemorative events have also been held online, allowing people from all over the world to participate and pay their respects. This global participation underscores the universal lessons and implications of the Chernobyl disaster.

Preserving the Memory:

The act of remembering Chernobyl extends beyond the physical monuments and annual events. Books, films, and documentaries have been produced, recounting the events, personal stories, and scientific facts surrounding the disaster. The 2019 HBO miniseries "Chernobyl" brought the story of the disaster and its heroes to a global audience, re-emphasizing the importance of remembering and learning from the past.

Memorialization and commemorative events honoring the victims of Chernobyl play a crucial role in acknowledging the human cost of the disaster, honoring the bravery of those who responded, and ensuring that the lessons of Chernobyl are not forgotten.

The Significance of Remembrance in Preventing Future Disasters

In the face of a disaster as profound as Chernobyl, remembrance serves a dual purpose. It offers a path for collective mourning and honoring the victims, while also standing as a crucial instrument in the prevention of future disasters. By keeping the memory of Chernobyl alive, we remind ourselves and future generations of the high cost of complacency, inadequate safety measures, and the unforgiving nature of nuclear power when mishandled.

Understanding the Past:

First and foremost, remembrance helps us to comprehend and acknowledge the gravity of what happened. The Chernobyl disaster was not simply an accident. It was a sequence of events marked by human error, flawed design, and a failure in leadership. Remembering the tragedy underlines these failures and reminds us of the importance of diligence, scrutiny, and accountability in the management of nuclear power.

Educating Future Generations:

Remembrance is also a vital educational tool. By studying the events leading up to the disaster, the response, and the long-term impact, we gain invaluable insights into the scope of nuclear risks. The Chernobyl story serves as a stark case study for nuclear engineers, policymakers, health professionals, and the public at large. It embodies the practical lessons of nuclear safety and disaster management that are pertinent even today.

Influencing Policy and Practice:

Remembering Chernobyl has had a profound impact on nuclear policy and practice worldwide. The disaster triggered a paradigm shift in the approach to nuclear safety, driving the implementation of stricter regulations, the design of safer reactors, and increased international cooperation on nuclear safety issues. By keeping the memory of Chernobyl alive, we reinforce the importance of these changes and the ongoing need for vigilance and transparency.

Fostering a Culture of Safety:

Beyond influencing policy, remembrance fosters a culture of safety. The haunting images of the abandoned city of Pripyat, the stories of the liquidators, and the ongoing health issues faced by the survivors make the abstract concept of nuclear disaster tangible and real. This cultural awareness of the risks is critical in encouraging a cautious and respectful approach to nuclear power and other potentially hazardous technologies.

The act of remembering Chernobyl serves as a safeguard against complacency, a tool for education, a driver for policy changes, and a catalyst for a culture of safety. It emphasizes the profound responsibility we carry in the harnessing of nuclear power and the imperative to protect future generations from a similar fate. As philosopher George Santayana famously stated, "Those who cannot remember the past are condemned to repeat it." In the case of Chernobyl, the cost of forgetting is simply too high.

OLIVER LANCASTER

Conclusion: Reflections on Chernobyl: Looking Back, Moving Forward

Summary of Key Takeaways and Lessons Learned from the Chernobyl Disaster

The Chernobyl disaster was a catastrophe that forever altered our understanding of nuclear power and its potential consequences. It stands as a grim testament to the dangers of complacency, poor design, and inadequate safety measures in the face of such a potent energy source. Reflecting on this event, we can distill several critical lessons:

1. Safety is Paramount:

Chernobyl highlighted the catastrophic consequences of lax safety protocols and flawed reactor design. Since then, stringent safety standards have become a cornerstone of nuclear power plant design and operation worldwide. This lesson extends beyond the nuclear industry, emphasizing that safety should never be compromised in any potentially hazardous enterprise.

2. Transparency is Essential:

The Soviet Union's initial attempt to downplay the disaster led to delayed international assistance and contributed to the spread of radiation beyond its borders. This incident underscored the need for transparency and honesty in dealing with such crises, particularly those with potential global implications.

3. Disaster Preparedness and Response:

Chernobyl showcased the importance of effective disaster preparedness and response strategies. The brave efforts of the liquidators were hampered by the lack of a comprehensive plan to handle such a disaster. Today, nations worldwide have emergency procedures in place, specifically tailored to deal with nuclear accidents.

4. Long-Term Health and Environmental Impacts:

The long-lasting health and environmental effects of the Chernobyl disaster have highlighted the need for ongoing monitoring and support in the aftermath of nuclear accidents. Health services for affected individuals and rigorous environmental remediation are integral parts of the response to such events.

5. The Human Cost:

The disaster at Chernobyl resulted not only in the immediate loss of life but also in long-term physical and psychological suffering for survivors. It underlined the immense human cost of nuclear accidents, emphasizing the necessity of robust safety measures and disaster response plans.

6. Community and Global Cooperation:

Lastly, Chernobyl illustrated the critical role of both local community support and global cooperation in disaster response and recovery. The successful containment of the site and support for the affected individuals involved both community initiatives and international assistance.

The Chernobyl disaster stands as a stark reminder of the high stakes involved in harnessing nuclear power. The lessons learned from this tragedy have reshaped the global nuclear industry, guided international policy, and influenced public perception. It is crucial that we keep these lessons in mind to prevent a recurrence of such a disaster in the future.

The Importance of Nuclear Safety and the Global Energy Landscape

The Chernobyl disaster, one of the most significant accidents in the history of nuclear energy production, has significantly influenced the global approach to nuclear safety and its place in the world's energy landscape. Its devastating consequences underlined the urgent need for comprehensive safety measures, stringent regulations, and transparent practices in nuclear power management.

Nuclear Safety: A Priority

The Chernobyl incident was a profound wakeup call for the international nuclear industry, highlighting the catastrophic potential when safety is compromised. The disaster reinforced the critical importance of nuclear safety at every stage, from the design of reactors to their operation, maintenance, and eventual decommissioning.

Safety in nuclear energy production involves a multitude of factors. These include physical safeguards, such as containment structures and shutdown systems, and procedural safeguards, such as regular inspections, staff training, emergency planning, and a robust regulatory framework.

The International Atomic Energy Agency (IAEA) and other global organizations have since ramped up efforts to strengthen nuclear safety standards worldwide, establishing guidelines for nations to follow.

The Global Energy Landscape: A Delicate Balance

Nuclear power has the potential to play a pivotal role in meeting global energy demand, especially given the growing concerns over climate change. It is a low-carbon power source, producing minimal greenhouse gases compared to fossil fuels. This advantage positions nuclear power as a viable part of the solution in the transition towards a sustainable energy mix.

However, the Chernobyl disaster serves as a stark reminder of the risks associated with nuclear power. It necessitates a careful balancing act: harnessing the benefits of nuclear energy while vigilantly managing the associated risks.

In the years following Chernobyl, some countries chose to reduce their reliance on nuclear power, while others continued to view it as a necessary component of their energy strategies, albeit with enhanced safety measures. The discussion around nuclear power remains a contentious issue in the global energy discourse.

The Path Forward

As we look towards the future of the global energy landscape, the lessons from Chernobyl must remain at the forefront. The disaster has underscored that while nuclear energy can be part of the solution to our energy needs, it requires an unyielding commitment to safety, regulation, and transparency.

Morcover, ongoing technological advances, such as the development of Generation IV reactors and small modular reactors (SMRs), promise enhanced safety features and lower waste production. These advancements, coupled with rigorous safety protocols, may help to mitigate the risks associated with nuclear power.

As we navigate the global energy landscape and seek sustainable, low-carbon power solutions, the legacy of Chernobyl continues to resonate. The importance of nuclear safety remains paramount, a lesson that has been written in the radioactive ashes of the Chernobyl disaster.

Sign up to my free newsletter to get updates on new releases, FREE teaser chapters to upcoming releases and FREE digital short stories.

Or visit https://tinyurl.com/olanc

I never spam and you can unsubscribe at any time.

Don't miss out!

Visit the website below and you can sign up to receive emails whenever Oliver Lancaster publishes a new book. There's no charge and no obligation.

https://books2read.com/r/B-A-UNEZ-FVYKC

BOOKS2READ

Connecting independent readers to independent writers.

Also by Oliver Lancaster

A Comprehensive Account of the Nuclear Disaster

About the Author

Oliver Lancaster possesses an enchanting charm that effortlessly draws readers into the depths of his literary world. With an insatiable curiosity for the unexplained, he skillfully weaves tales of crime, conspiracy, mystery and the unknown, leaving readers on the edge of their seats.

Nestled away in the seclusion of his garden shed, Oliver finds solace and inspiration in the tranquility of nature. Surrounded by greenery and fragrant blooms, he dives into a realm of imagination, unearthing secrets that lie hidden within his mind.

Accompanying Oliver on his literary ventures is his faithful ginger cat named Italics. With his mesmerizing gaze and mysterious mannerisms, Italics adds an air of intrigue to Oliver's writing process, often curling up on a cushioned chair nearby, watching as words flow effortlessly from his human companion's pen.

When not engrossed in his craft, Oliver indulges in the gentle warmth of his garden with a glass of red wine.

Prepare to be spellbound as you delve into the pages of Oliver Lancaster's novels, for he is a master of the eerie, a weaver of secrets, and an unrivaled guide through the labyrinthine corridors of the human psyche.

Sign up to a free newsletter to get updates on new releases, FREE teaser chapters to upcoming releases and FREE digital short stories.

Read more at https://tinyurl.com/olanc.

www.ingramcontent.com/pod-product-compliance
Lightning Source LLC
Chambersburg PA
CBHW051211160726
47994CB00002B/553